New York Central
Color Photography of Ed Nowak

Book 1
by Ed Nowak
with Robert J. Yanosey

Published by
Morning Sun Books, Inc.
11 Sussex Court
Edison, N.J. 08820
Library of Congress Catalog Card Number: 91-067986
Typesetting by R. J. Yanosey of Morning Sun Books.

First Printing
ISBN 1-878887-09-2

Ed Nowak and editor/publisher Bob Yanosey at Rochester station on the former NYC main, September 12, 1991.

Dedication

This book is dedicated to my wife Ruth Nowak, who spent many a night alone while I photographed the large area of the New York Central System.

Table of Contents

Introduction

Throughout the various decades of American railroading, no name of an official company photographer is more famous than that of Ed Nowak. During the 1940's and 50's, his artistry and skill with the camera fashioned the image of the New York Central Railroad, an image which became *our* image of the road. When the talk turns to the *Water Level Route* in railfan circles, unconsciously the mind conjures up one of Nowak's classic scenes: a Mohawk with a string of *Pacemaker* box cars at Breakneck Mountain, the new TWENTIETH CENTURY LIMITED in 1948 along the Hudson, the looking-straight-down "Beehive" photo of the information booth at Grand Central. His lens saw what we came to know and love as a refined mixture of sleek two-tone grey streamliners and fast merchandise freights gliding effortlessly along multi-tracked "water-level" rights-of-way. The Central certainly made a propitious decision when it hired Ed Nowak in 1941.

Edwin S. Nowak was born on April 18, 1918, appropriately enough, deep in Central territory outside Rochester, N.Y. In this Kodak-dominated city, photography was a popular hobby, one which young Ed soon fell in love with and used to his advantage to obtain his early jobs. Making his way to New York City, he managed to convince the New York Central that hiring him would prove to be most beneficial to both parties. Fortunately, they agreed.

Ed's long and quite distinguished tour of duty with the New York Central has been meticulously related in the book *Ed Nowak's NEW YORK CENTRAL* by Ed Nowak with Karl Zimmerman, published by PTJ Publishing, Inc. in 1983. His full NYC story and entire background is examined thoroughly therein, complete with several hundred of his famous black and white photos. We have avoided repeating information already relayed in that fine effort. What most people do not real-

ize is that often Ed also took color views of the NYC during this period; photographs that, because of printing limitations during the forties and fifties, have rarely been seen. Those photos are the basis of this album and its two companions to follow about a year apart. Some will be quite familiar, old friends, that you will marvel at as you see them for the first time in full color. Others have not been seen before, even in black and white. They are reproduced from Ed's original 4 x 5" transparencies.

When all three albums are finished a limited number of embossed slip-cases will also be made available to contain the set and enable the collector to shelve the series either vertically or horizontally on his bookcase.

In presenting the work on these pages, we have felt that our utmost responsibility was to preserve the color of these transparencies forever through this printing. The urgency of this is quite evident in some of the transparencies from the mid fifties and early sixties which are losing their color due to unstable film. Some of these faded pictures are included in small formats for continuity and completeness. Fortunately the more numerous Kodachrome film used in the forties and fifties looks like it was taken yesterday and forms the foundation for this, Ed's color photography album. So sit back and look over Ed Nowak's shoulder as he narrates his recollections about taking these memorable pictures. Enjoy a photographic tribute to a young professional photographer shooting assignments for his corporate client. And see how his interpretation of those assignments sculpted your concept of the New York Central RR.

Robert J. Yanosey

November 7, 1991

Harmon

What I learned about railroading was strictly "on the job." I was, and still am, a camera buff. I love photography. When I first arrived in New York City I started to work for a photographer who worked for *Vogue Magazine*, which was involved in fashions. Working for these people made me uncomfortable as they were not the same sort of folks I was used to in Rochester. I just didn't like the atmosphere. At the time my job was located at 480 Lexington Avenue along with forty-seven other studios. This was the very hub of photography in this country at the time. Right next door was the New York Central, a door which I soon started knocking on hoping to get in.

The Central never had a real photographer. They had one fellow, Dave Hyde, who had been a high school and college basketball star. At that time, the railroad used athletes like Dave, Stella Walsh and others to carry the New York Central insignia in sport events. They would give them a job, a make-up job. Stella Walsh was hired as a secretary in Cleveland and probably spent two days a year at the office, the rest of the time in field and track events. Dave was a basketball star hired as a messenger in the NYC photo department. Whatever he learned he picked up from the former sports star ahead of him. In the forties they were still going out with flash powder making those huge puffs of smoke. For something special like an annual report, the road called in a professional photographer by the name of Ivan Dmitri at a rate of about $700 a day. That $700 figure was my ticket onto the New York Central. That, and the fact I could shoot color.

Croton Harmon, NY was a "natural" for NYC photography. Close to both my New York City office and home, I took photos there over a span of five different decades. Here some of the new diesels are bringing a freight past the shops in 1967 toward the end of the Central era.

This is a "set-up" photo of a new diesel in Harmon Yard in April 1948 when they were still a novelty. It was probably taken for use in an annual report or some railroad magazine.

While at Harmon one day on another assignment, I happened by these
steam locomotives and knew I had a good photo opportunity.

We always need pictures to augment our files, and occasionally during my vacation I'd use my week off and take my car to cover a different division. I'd possibly go out to parts of the Big Four and scout location shots for future pictures. While there I'd speak to the Road Foreman of Engines or Superintendent and ask if there was anything noteworthy they thought needed photography while I was out here. Sometimes they would come up with a subject, sometimes they didn't. Of course, as the official company photographer, if I wanted something moved, they'd move it for me.

Of course, there was a constant need for photos of the new diesels back in the forties. They were the figurative embodiment of modern railroading of the time. These two were taken at Harmon in May 1948. When we took photos like these we would ask the shop to clean up the engine. Now with black, all they had to do was spray black paint. With the other one, they would wash it first, and then do some matching of colors so the patchwork of color didn't show up in the photo.

While taking pictures of these engines in the yard, our biggest problem was sometimes the hostler didn't want to move the engine beyond a certain switch point. He would say: "When I go beyond that point, I get a day's pay for road work." So I had to avoid pushing him out onto the mainline to get the proper lighting or to steer clear of extraneous space or distracting details.

New lightning striped E7's at Harmon in April 1947.

The lightning stripe scheme was expensive to apply and by the early sixties was to be eliminated. These three E8's were painted black, green and grey as a test in September 1961 at Harmon. Grey won.

This was one of the big, new Niagara class engines. We wanted a photo to emphasize that bigness, so we had one of the hostlers get up on top and make believe he was cleaning the headlight so that it would compare the size of the engine to his height (especially those huge elephant ears beside him).

For a long time the New York Central didn't want to use this photo of the Niagara taken from the Harmon roundhouse roof. This was June of 1945 and it was one of the first that came in without the elephant ears, a fact which made the road reject this photo.

The Hudson 4-6-4 was symbolic of the New York Central and naturally turned up in a lot of my photos. This is a study of the side rods of a Hudson taken at Harmon in 1946. The brass had been oiled and cleaned making a nice composition for the camera.

There was coal soot inches deep on the roundhouse roof at Harmon during World War II, and I got awfully dirty taking this photo. Hudson #5326 takes a ride on the turntable on November 11, 1944 . . . a dirty, but extremely effective part of the nation's war effort which was churning away at full tilt. Hitler and Roosevelt were still alive, B29's were dropping bombs on Japan and the Battle of the Bulge was but a month away.

We tried to give life to static poses of diesels in the yard by posing people around them. NYC #4201 at Harmon in June 1951 was just another road diesel to me. Today, railfans revere the elegant Alco PA, a streamlined passenger locomotive with 2000 horses inside.

The 1931 Lionel train catalogue had a cover showing NYC engineer Bob Butterfield in front of the drivers of his Hudson showing a new 400E model steamer to two young boys. Seventeen years later in 1948 and continuing for eight years, the Lionel Company began production of another of its most famous models, the lightning striped New York Central F3. The Lionel publicity department wanted a photograph of a boy beside a real locomotive of ours so that they could run it in an ad showing him playing with the Lionel model. The boy is D.V. Hyde, Jr., son of our fellow photographer Dave Hyde. He is comparing time with engineer George Dennis at Harmon on January 13, 1951.

Harmon was also used to pose passengers using our trains. Unlike other suburban Hudson Division stations, all through trains stopped at Harmon. This is September 1946 and models are boarding new Pullman-Standard cars.

The same day, our models show the fashionable way to dress and travel. In 1946, train travel was still glamourous, a much more formal affair than today.

No model here as a NYC conductor gives a "high ball" at Harmon station in November 1944. Neither was this posed, but merely a portrait showing the age-old routine of a working conductor.

Model Connie Russell posing for a calender shot marking the 1650th diesel obtained by the Central. The date was April 3, 1952 and the thought was to put the year *1953* into the vacated numberboard.

Employees at work were subjects always in demand for company publications. These photos would often run in a series showing workers at different locations doing the same task. We had series of pictures on men working on steam locomotives, overhauling them and brightening up their appearance. Later we did much the same with diesels. These two men are cleaning this engine's drivers at Harmon.

An employee fills a tender with water in November 1944, while seven years later in June 1951 heavy repairs are underway in a diesel.

At one time we received a request from a member of the New York Central Board of Director's for a picture of a moving TWENTIETH CENTURY LIMITED for use on his letterhead. Well, showing a moving steam locomotive was no problem because you almost always get the plume of smoke behind. But, how do you show a moving diesel? I set out to experiment using the image of an Indianapolis race car and its blur going behind the front end of the car. I tried to achieve this with a diesel backing up while the shutter was open on a camera mounted on a tripod. Finally, we did decide how to simulate speeding diesels, but in the meantime we had unfortunate test results like this one in Harmon June 26, 1951.

Normal images of streamlined trains
(September 1946) and diesel 4024
(April 1948) were rather routine.

Weehawken

Another NYC field location in close proximity to my New York office was Weehawken, NJ which had the added attraction of a big time freight operation. These three December 1948 views show the Weehawken Yard and the Hudson River which separates it from New York City. The focus of business today is the unloading of bauxite ore.

Bauxite was not the only commodity transferred from water to rail at Weehawken. Here on May 20, 1947 wood pulp is unloaded from a Norwegian ship at Pier 9.

In 1964 an experiment was conducted testing the feasibility of loading ships with containers taken directly from railroad flat cars.

In August 1972 at Weehawken, Seatrain containers are hoisted off flat cars in a more conventional way.

Weehawken was the center of New York Central's maritime fleet. All kinds of NYC tugs, barges, ferries and other vessels were to be found here on any given day. Here in April 1948, barges are repaired in the company of some idle commuter ferries, while in the smaller photo in July 1950, tugs gather at the Marine Shop.

On a cold but clear January 16, 1952, two Central tugs are tied up in front of Pier 2 Weehawken.

NYC tugs and barges keep company with Swedish ships just after world hostilities ceased in September 1945.

Of course, Weehawken wasn't merely concerned with maritime operations. Here the railroad had a firm beachhead for its freight operation to service the busy New York marketplace. In April 1950, an employee takes a wrench to the roof of an Alco diesel switcher while symbolically enough, steam shoulders on in the background.

Taken from high up on the palisades, Weehawken presents itself as a very busy place in June 1947. It was the terminus of the NYC West Shore line where commuters used the road's ferries to scurry back and forth across the Hudson.

There was also steam to be photographed at Weehawken. In January 1951, Boston & Albany #585 and a few inches of snow create a study in white. This was unusual for a B&A locomotive to stray down here to New Jersey.

Two years earlier on a much nicer day in April 1949, a Mohawk prepares to depart up the West Shore while a Jersey Central transfer waits alongside. The Mohawk is facing directly south, but would shortly make a complete 180 degree turn to the north utilizing the Weehawken Tunnel. It would continue its trip along the west shore of the Hudson River, with an ultimate destination of Selkirk Yard just outside Albany. The CNJ camelback would maintain a southerly heading along the National Docks Branch to reach its home terminal in nearby Jersey City.

33

Putnam Division

The Putnam Division was a quiet suburban line branching north out of New York City to Chatham, NY. Briarcliff Manor was a typical affluent station served by steam-drawn passenger trains like this June 1951 scene.

I lived on-line in Yorktown Heights, so I naturally picked-up a shot of this unusual load in September 1951. The "Put" was the best all-rail route into New York City for high and wide loads. The huge girder was being hauled by locomotive #1244, a 4-6-0.

The "Put" roundhouse was at White Plains, NY where this scene of the tenders sticking out intrigued me in June 1945.

On the mainline, the Central had water pans, but on all the side tracks they still had to fill up the tender at a water tank. In Yorktown Heights in June 1951, the classic pose of a hostler waiting for the tank to fill is fixed in time forever.

With all five thousand gallons aboard, the next thing to do is turn the engine for the return trip. You needed two or three men to get the "armstrong" turntable turned by hand in Yorktown Heights.

Empire State Express

The EMPIRE STATE EXPRESS was perhaps the Central's second best known passenger train after the TWENTIETH CENTURY LIMITED. As such the NYC publicity department was always in need of photographs of the train, and not just train photos either, but ones that covered all aspects of equipment, service and decor.

The railroad commissioned some paintings to use as advertisements for the EMPIRE STATE EXPRESS and I was asked to copy them in color for use as posters. They then were used on company calenders, advertisements, timetables and brochures. The horizontal format poster was done by Helck and copied in 1949. The two vertical posters were products of Leslie Ragan.

The EMPIRE STATE EXPRESS had two J3 Hudsons specially streamlined to match the fluted Budd consist of 1941. They were distinctive, modern looking engines, perfect for a pretty girl to pose on.

Westbound out of Albany, NY, Central trains had to fight their way up one of the few hills on the *Water Level Route*. Of course, no mention was ever made of the hill when the photograph was used. This is the EMPIRE STATE EXPRESS in April 1946 at the site of the old Mohawk & Hudson inclined planes.

Streamlined Super Hudson #5429 arrives and poses for the camera. The silver fluting which matched the consist of the EMPIRE STATE EXPRESS added one more touch of class to an already strikingly handsome locomotive.

By 1947, diesels were the "latest thing" and we needed updated publicity views of the **EMPIRE STATE EXPRESS.** On October 22, 1947 we arranged to take a set-up photo of the dieselized train at Lyons, NY. At that time, I believe we had to be in Lyons because they were going to work on a new Centralized Traffic Control tower in the area, so we decided to make this picture there and "kill two birds with one stone."

The following month we had another "two for one" opportunity present itself. This is Little Falls, NY in November 1947 showing the first train (EMPIRE STATE EXPRESS) going over the new Little Falls curve.

This had always been a dangerous spot. In April 1940, the LAKE SHORE LIMITED derailed here going around Gulf curve at excessive speed killing thirty-one people. Since then the area had always been subject to a slow speed restriction. To remedy the situation the railroad wanted to encroach upon both the Erie canal and Mohawk River here but never could receive permission. Finally, proper authorization to fill in a portion of the waterways was received and the curve was made less acute raising the track speed.

EMPIRE STATE EXPRESS cars were specially built for that train and assigned names of New York State governors. In January 1945, I photographed the interior of the entire train producing these views of a coach, the observation *Franklin Roosevelt*, and a parlor car.

Sometimes we photographed actual passengers on trains, sometimes models. If they were passengers we had to ask each one in the picture for permission. Sometimes a male passenger did not want his wife to know he was traveling to Albany that day when he had told her he was going down to Washington, DC. Most of the time we used models, and to a lesser degree, railroad employees.

In September 1946, service on the EMPIRE STATE EXPRESS dining car is portrayed in these two views.

The uniformed hostess aboard the EMPIRE STATE EXPRESS assists a passenger in 1950.

The three "passengers" in the front are models while NYC office staff fills up the rest of the observation car in this posed scene at Mott Haven Yard in June 1943.

$$\textit{Poughkeepsie}$$

Up on the Hudson Division at the very end of the commuter district, the town of Poughkeepsie had a large crushed stone outfit right next to our tracks. The background appealed to me and we began thinking of either an EMPIRE STATE EXPRESS or TWENTIETH CENTURY LIMITED photo at this site. Before making arrangements for posed trains, we went up and took some preliminary angles we thought interesting in May 1946.

In February 1957, I returned to the New York Trap Rock plant in Poughkeepsie to photograph the EMPIRE STATE EXPRESS and a freight train. The northbound EMPIRE STATE EXPRESS came by and made the stop as instructed. We had two problems. First the freight hadn't arrived yet, and second, the steam escaping from the rear car was threatening to obliterate the rear view of the passenger train. Finally after a few minutes, everything clicked and so did my camera. The EXPRESS was released without too much delay.

Twelve years earlier on March 4, 1945, the Ektar 127mm lens on my *Speed Graphic* stopped a freight coming through Poughkeepsie proper.

$$\mathcal{Boston}$$

New York Central served New England via its Boston & Albany extension. Usually when I went up to Boston from our New York office I took the New Haven, rather than the more roundabout all-New York Central routing. It was simply a lot faster. This is the B&A mainline and freight yard at Beacon Park, Boston on June 8, 1946. On the opposite page, there is a "bird's eye" view of South Station, Boston and its coach yards.

Two spring trips up to Boston resulted in these views of the Exeter Street coach yard in June 1949 and on the opposite page, May 1951.

The signal bridge crossing the throat of South Station, Boston interested me since it was unusual in having letters instead of numbers. In December 1946 I photographed some signal maintainers working up high among the semaphores. While there, two of our Mohawks answered the call of the blades and moved under the huge bridge.

In April 1945, I was in Boston composing some views of a rather mundane subject. This was a grain elevator in Boston Harbor that the company wanted some pictures of for some reason. Sadly, my trip was cut short with the news to return to New York City promptly and prepare for photography of President Roosevelt's funeral train.

Mohawk Valley

I had a number of published views like these taken in the Mohawk Valley near Fonda and Herkimer, NY that might have formed the basis for this poster of Central trains painted by Helck in 1949. I remember when Dave Hyde and I went up to that area in the late forties we had a specific request to try and get a high vantage point to look down on our railroad and the Mohawk River. Dave had heard that there were lots of snakes up in those hills and he wouldn't set foot out of the car. I put on these high top boots and accompanied by one of our maintenance foremen went up and shot these photos. Finally, when we finished and came down off Big Nose Mountain, the foreman muttered to me and Dave that he "would like to show us something." There behind his nearby garage he had a "pen" with about a dozen rattlesnakes inside. Chewing on a piece of grass, he casually added: "They all came from that hill."

Even heavy tonnage freight had an easy time of it along the *Water Level Route*. The publicity department liked to emphasize the lack of grades inherent in our moniker, so rivers were often prominent in our publicity photos as was the four track main which enhanced that fluid look.

Fall arrives in the Mohawk Valley at Little Falls, NY.

By the time of the merger in 1968, the New York Central was a much different railroad than it had been right after World War II. The old image was that of a speeding Hudson flying down a four track main with a long passenger consist trailing behind. By August 21, 1967 when this maintenance photo was taken, the road had been dieselized for ten years and was busy cutting back on surplus main tracks wherever they existed. The Central was cutting costs by mechanizing its labor-intensive track work such as this tie gang using the Kirshaw tie inserting machine on the once four track main in the Mohawk Valley at North Ilion, NY.

Flexi-Van

In the late 1950's, while most other American railroads were ballyhooing truck-on-train piggyback service, the Central developed and stuck with its own concept called *Flexi-Van*. Simply put, *Flexi-Van* was a container which could ride on truck bogey wheels on the road or be carried on special flat cars without the wheels. This was especially important to the Central which was plagued by low clearances on its east end. As you might expect, I put in a lot of time photographing this unique service for the road.

North Bergen, NJ *Flexi-Van* terminal in April 1958. *Flexi-Van* had been thoroughly tested in 1957 and regular service had been inaugurated this month. By the mid-sixties, *Flexi-Van* traffic grew to over 150,000 vans a year and pioneer terminals like North Bergen had to be greatly expanded.

A refrigerated *Flexi-Van* is loaded onto one of the road's special cars for that service.

"Commando" unit turning *Flexi-Van* trailer at North Bergen in 1963.

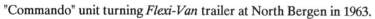

New York Central was the only east-west trunk line which managed to take its freight operation directly into New York City by rail. *Flexi-Van* offered the road another method of penetrating this market and the road established a terminal for the service in The Bronx at High Bridge Yard. Since *Flexi-Van* was a real novelty and needed the concept explained, much of my film was expended to show our shippers and stockholders how the vans were handled and swung onto the special flat cars. Co-ordinated rail-highway-water scheduling of *Flexi-Vans* helped Central make the service one of its true growth businesses.

Late in the afternoon a *Flexi-Van* train is made up under the famous aqueduct viaduct in The Bronx. High Bridge was once the electric-steam change point in the early part of the century.

By 1966, Central had developed so much *Flexi-Van* traffic that it was operating twelve dedicated trains called *Super-Vans*. To photograph the hot *Super-Van* trains out on the road, we chose one of our favorite locales, Bannerman's Island and an unusual perspective from atop Breakneck Mountain at Cold Spring, NY.

We were always trying to show something else beside the train in our photos. These photos were made for a cover of *Modern Railroads* magazine and the 1961 Annual Report. We were attempting to show off our *Flexi-Van* service, of course, but also the ability of our mechanized track work to continue uninterrupted on a parallel main while a train passed.

A *Super-Van* passes over another Central improvement, a hot box detector in this series of photographs made at Bergen, NY in 1960. In June 1961, *Trains Magazine* named NYC's *Super-Van* train as the world's first freight to run faster than a mile a minute from start to final terminal.

Just east of Rochester, NY, the Central maintained a large coaling and watering facility for steam locomotives directly on the mainline. I visited Wayneport in November 1945 to capture these views of Hudson #5272 with a passenger train and two Mohawks with freights.

In March 1946, Mikado #1599 advances its hopper train around Wayneport curve before refreshing itself, while in November 1945 the head brakeman stands on the tender of Mohawk #2969 as it moves slowly up to the water plugs.

Rochester

Rochester, NY is well represented in my repertoire of New York Central photographs because at the time I was courting my wife-to-be who lived in that city. I used all kinds of excuses to go up to Wayneport or Dispatch Shops for photography.

The ADVANCE EMPIRE STATE EXPRESS has Niagara #6024 this day in November 1949 as it sweeps into Rochester station.

The railroad rebuilt part of the interior of the station at Rochester, so in September 1944 I had a legitimate reason to visit the city. The new "Ladies' Lounge" is in striking contrast to the stark decor of today's stations.

A rear view of the EMPIRE STATE EXPRESS at Rochester station in April 1945.

Out by Wayneport coaling station, a beautiful white plume is added to the snowy scene.

December 1944 was an especially bad winter around Rochester. The road stationed some "protect" engines at the station like this Pacific veiled in steam, while a Mohawk works by on the main. This is approximately the same spot where the page two photo was taken forty-seven years later.

A fork lift picks up five freight car wheels to take into the shop in this February 1957 photo.

The New York Central had a subsidiary called Despatch Shops which handled most of the road's freight car building and repairs. It was located in East Rochester. In order to perform its assignment, Despatch Shops had many stockpiles of car materials which became subjects for my employees-at-work series of photos. Here material is loaded onto a forklift in June 1957.

Freight car axles were stacked thirteen high in June 1957.

Truck frames are piled up outside Despatch Shops by a crane with a magnet in February 1957.

Welding the huge underframes of freight cars under construction was a particularly interesting subject in Despatch Shops. On March 16, 1956 the work was being performed in special positioning jigs.

On March 16, 1956 apprentice John Hamm is seen welding a car sill and then at the flash arc welder. This was part of a series of photographs for the New York Central employee magazine concerning the training of new employees.

Eventually it was time for the finished product to leave the plant. In February 1957, the Despatch Shop switcher poses with a half dozen new *Early Bird* box cars. *Early Bird* was a NYC freight service which cut a full day off shipment time between Chicago and the East.

We were always in need of good freight train pictures. Unfortunately, you couldn't depend on a regular freight to look as neat and modern as the company would have it. When Despatch Shops released its daily output of cars they were switched into any regular train and a photograph might also show some old junk that the company wouldn't like shown in a national publication. So we began to ask Despatch to hold three or four day's worth of production so that a solid train might be assembled for photography. In June 1946, the shop was producing covered hoppers and this special was photographed just west of Rochester in the town of Churchville.

On August 10, 1947, Despatch Shops was building refrigerator cars for another NYC subsidiary, Merchant's Dispatch Transportation Corporation. We photographed these trains at Churchville, NY just west of Rochester because the Central always took actual delivery of the new cars at Erie, PA which provided a tax advantage over New York State. The biggest change in this year's photo was not so much the cars behind but the changeover to diesel. As you can see, however, steam managed to "still be in the picture."

Several months later on October 16, 1947, Despatch was running 40-foot box cars and again we arrived to record the event at Churchville.

Whenever we had a "set-up" photo like this we would take a number of views of the posed train in both black and white and color. I always appreciated the symetrical look of a uniform train consist.

Ice

As you can see in this August 1947 photo of a new refrigerator train at Churchville, the MDT reefers had their roof hatches open to allow air in during this initial westbound trip. The hatches were used to load cakes of ice into bunkers inside the cars providing a suitable cold temperature during transit of perishables.

Covering the consist with crushed ice was another method used to keep the perishables cold. The employee on the wood deck is guiding a cake of ice into a mobile machine which would crush it and send it through the hose which the other employee is deploying into the reefer. In this May 1949 case, MDT #47352 is having its California lettuce "top-iced" at the Indiana Harbor Belt Yard in Blue Island, just outside Chicago. Both MDT and IHB were Central subsidiaries.

The New York Central was involved in many things which didn't appear
to be associated with running trains. In Carthage, NY, the road had a
private lake available for ice harvesting before the age of mechanical
refrigeration. These are two scenes from January 1947 showing the
preparation and actual harvest that winter. The Central would then
transport it to a warehouse, put straw in between the layers and have it
available just about the entire year for re-icing at Wayneport.

Ohio

In Ohio, the New York Central spread out to the south and west, networking the *Buckeye State*. The town of Bellefontaine was the hub of the Central subsidiary Cleveland, Cincinnati, Chicago & St. Louis or "Big Four" as it was more commonly known. On November 9, 1949 we visited in order to pose a freight passing the Bellefontaine freight station which had *Pacemaker* LCL service.

Up on Lake Erie, Astabula was a very busy NYC port that handled both iron ore and coal for the Central. Coal from western Pennsylvania was shipped out here and iron ore like this was fed into our hoppers for delivery to Youngstown or the P&LE. In the middle of this route was Carson Hill, a factor which coerced the *Water Level Route* into breaking its own precedent by purchasing dynamic brake equipped GP7's. Astabula itself was more noteworthy in NYC history because of a tragic affair on December 29, 1876 when the Lake Shore's PACIFIC EXPRESS collapsed the Astabula Creek bridge, killing ninety-two.

103

Toledo, Ohio was also on the Central at the western tip of Lake Erie.
We had occasion to visit the city in November 1950 when the new Central
Union Terminal was opened. The Central built it to replace a relic of a
station and then leased space to B&O, C&O and Wabash.

We found out that some people didn't know what it meant when "employees were working down in the pit." So we decided to show them what the pit was and chose Stanley Shops in Toledo as a studio. This looking-up-from-the-pit photo of F3 #1611 was taken in January 1953.

On July 22-23, 1966, the New York Central made its famous high speed test runs with a jet engine-equipped RDC at Bryan, OH. At the time there had been a lot of publicity about "Bullet" trains in Japan and the Central felt obligated to demonstrate what could be done here in the United States. After several test runs on the straight stretch of track at Bryan, the jazzy Budd car was able to reach 183 MPH. One of the jets broke down after that trip but the engineers wanted to repair it and break 200 MPH the next day. Top management had a press conference already scheduled, however, so despite the begging of the Tech Center engineers, they were told to return to their regular assignments. My job had been to take pictures of the entire operation, especially the special powder on the tracks to show wheel adhesion. They wanted to make sure the thing wasn't riding on air above the rails!

Jets & Trucks

Despite a systematic year-by-year slashing of the *Great Steel Fleet* that had begun in the fifties, by 1966 the Central was still losing over $15 million a year on long distance passenger service. The NYC marketing department determined that most inter-city travel on its trains was under 200 miles a trip and began an effort to re-structure the service accordingly. Part of this effort involved a test of a high speed rail car developed by Central's Cleveland Technical Center.

The Central had a more sincere interest in a more practical vehicle, the truck. It was the means of escaping the boundaries of the rail, a method to exploit the newer industries which had grown up outside the reach of a local siding. In the case of *Flexi-Van,* it also meant the ability to transload into ships for overseas destinations.

At the other end of our system and after the *Flexi-Van* image was changed into jade green, a truck was spotted in front of the St. Louis arch.

A Sheridan & Duncan pick up truck for New York Central
LCL business poses twenty years earlier in May 1947. Despite
the NYC logo, this was not a Central subsidiary.

Elkhart

On March 6, 1958, the New York Central dedicated its new yard at Elkhart, IN to Robert R. Young, the flamboyant financier who wrested control of the Central for himself in the early fifties only to commit suicide several years later. The road was very proud of the modern sciences applied to the new yard and had publicity photos taken from all angles including this aerial.

The key ingredient of the yard was the operation of the hump which was run with a bank of computers. They controlled the track switches and retarders speeding movement of freight car classification.

The hump was busy day and night. The long nighttime exposure in February 1958 allowed just the right amount of blur to show the movement of the box car down the hump.

Inside the hump tower at Robert R. Young Yard, an analog computer would determine the speed of the car to be humped based on its weight, type, and distance to the next car on the destination track. The airport "look" was exactly the modern image the Central was hoping to create. Ten years earlier it had been simply a diesel, now electronics, computers, and radar were all a part of the modern railroad of 1958.

A *Super-Van* train comes into Elkhart to have its portrait taken in the middle of the night. The local operations people were terribly upset about doing this photo and prevailed upon us to stay out of the hump yard and on this run-around track. Even then they kept on pushing us to finish up. This part of the yard was completely dark and time was consumed moving some big portable lights around to illuminate the side of the train.

Central was also deeply concerned with Centralized Traffic Control (CTC) which eliminated many towers and much inherent expense. It went hand-in-hand with the track reductions which were being carried out system-wide. This is the operator at his CTC board in Terre Haute, IN in June 1959.

Exhibits

The New York Central had several pieces of historic equipment which were available for exhibition at special occasions. The very first locomotive of the New York Central System was the *De Witt Clinton* which was built in March 1831. The *Clinton* together with three stagecoach-type passenger cars made a historic journey from Albany to Schenectady on August 9, 1831. The trip was concluded at such discomfort that after a year the *Clinton* was dismantled. In 1892, this replica was created by West Albany Shops and began a lifetime career of exhibitions for the railroad, this being the Chicago Railroad Fair on July 22, 1948.

An epochal locomotive in the cavalcade of power progress on New York Central reads one of the posters at this 1951 celebration of the Corning, NY centennial.

Old #999 was undoubtedly Central's most famous individual locomotive. The 4-4-0 had the honor of racing the EMPIRE STATE EXPRESS along at the unheard of speed of 112.5 MPH on May 10, 1893. Saved from scrapping, the spit and polish locomotive was also at the Chicago Railroad Fair in 1948.

The Pacemaker

People tend to think of NYC passenger service between New York and Chicago only in terms of the TWENTIETH CENTURY LIMITED. The CENTURY was only one part of the road's *Great Steel Fleet*. The list of names reaches into the dozens, but one unsung train was THE PACEMAKER, an all-coach train which departed Chicago as #2 at 2:30 in the afternoon or Grand Central as #1 at 4:10 PM.

As quick as the Central could buy them, THE PACEMAKER like all the other members of the *Great Steel Fleet* was handed over to diesels like E7 #4028 seen here being prepared at Harmon in 1948.

While THE PACEMAKER was advertised as all-coach train, that was an understatement since it also carried an observation car, a dining car, and a kitchen lounge like this Budd-built car that I photogrpahed in Mott Haven in September 1947. THE PACEMAKER even advertised a coach reserved *for women only* New York to Chicago.

THE PACEMAKER was equipped with a dining car built by Budd Company. With venetian blinds drawn to avoid picking up any hint of the Mott Haven Yard photo locale, I recorded the interior both with and without models.

Pretty models aboard THE PACEMAKER's diner and kitchen lounge in September 1947. While we had tried on several occasions to save the company money by using office employees, professional models were much easier to work with and the results better.

La Salle St. Station

The New York Central terminated in Chicago at La Salle Street Station which was also occupied by two other railroads. One was the Rock Island which also operated long distance service in addition to commuter trains like this example I photographed in 1962. The other line was Nickel Plate which paralleled the Central all the way to Buffalo. On July 23, 1948 while waiting for NYC J3 Hudson #5445 to depart, I photographed one of their trains arriving the station.

One day I was to accompany a newspaper writer aboard the engine on the TWENTIETH CENTURY LIMITED leaving La Salle Street for a feature article which would gain our road some excellent free publicity. I was taking a picture of the writer boarding our engine when the conductor walked up front to compare watches with the engineer. Since it was necessary for the newspaperman to have a ticket because of an ICC requirement, he produced it at that time for the conductor. After examining it, the old conductor let us know exactly whose turf we were on by proclaiming: "This is no good here. This is a coach ticket and the TWENTIETH CENTURY has no coaches." In order not to embarass the newspaperman and the railroad, I had to produce sufficient cash on the spot to upgrade the ticket to roomette even though he spent the entire trip in the locomotive cab!

- THE WOLVERINE, THE PACEMAKER, the NEW ENGLAND STATES, THE COMMODORE VANDERBILT, the TWENTIETH CENTURY LIMITED, at La Salle Street October 23, 1949.